KV-515-701

Food Safety and Farming

ANDREA CLAIRE HARTE SMITH

FRANKLIN WATTS
LONDON • SYDNEY

R

23906S

NORTH EAST WORCESTERSHIRE
COLLEGE LIBRARY

363. 192 SMI

First published in 2002 by Franklin Watts
96 Leonard Street, London EC2A 4XD

Franklin Watts Australia
56 O'Riordan Street
Alexandria, NSW 2015

Copyright © Franklin Watts 2002

Series editor: Rachel Cooke
Series design: White Design
Picture research: Diana Morris

A CIP catalogue record for this book is available from the British Library.

ISBN 0 7496 4438 9

Dewey Classification 631.5

Printed in Belgium

Whilst every attempt has been made to clear copyright, should there
be any inadvertent omission, please apply in the first instance
to the publisher regarding rectification.

Acknowledgements:
Pete Addis/Environmental Images: 9b. Sarah Blackstock/Still Pictures: 26b.
Brogdale Horticultural Trust: 18t. Robert Brook/Environmental Images: 7b.
Nick Cobbing/Still Pictures: 22b. Nigel Dickinson/Still Pictures: 6b, 12b.
EPA/PA Photos: 29b. Peter Frischmuth/Still Pictures: 8t.
Dylan Garcia/Still Pictures: 13t. Patrik Giardino/Corbis: 5b.
Ron Giling/Still Pictures: 21b. H Giradet/Environmental Images: 20t.
David Hoffman/Environmental Images: 17b. Robert Holmgren/Still Pictures: 25t.
Image Quest/NHPA: 23c. Makoto Iwafuji/SPL: 28cl.
E A Janes/NHPA: 9c. Juliette Lasserre/Hulton Archive: 4t.
K Preston-Mafham/Premaphotos: 10b. Peter Menzel/SPL: 23t.
Ingrid Moorjohn/Still Pictures: 19b. Sean Murphy/Stone: 28tr.
Ralph Orlowski/Reuters/Popperfoto: front cover, 27b. PA Photos: 17t.
Thomas Raupach/Still Pictures: 16t. Hartmut Schwartzbach/Still Pictures: 24.
Soil Association: 11t. Andrew Syred/SPL: 14t.

WITHDRAWN

WITHDRAWN

WITHDRAWN

newcollege learning resources

239065   RA

CONTENTS

A FOOD REVOLUTION

GIVE A HOUSEWIFE *from the Fifties a tour of your home and she would probably be as amazed by the contents of your fridge as by your PC or mobile. Frozen pizza, exotic fruit, even orange juice would astound her. In the past 50 years, there has been a food revolution – and it's not just the contents of your fridge that have changed but shopping, food preparation and farming too.*

Fifties housewives would have shopped at small stores like this one rather than a supermarket.

DOWN THE SHOPS

Most Fifties housewives used to go shopping daily – they didn't have freezers. Supermarkets didn't exist, so they went to several stores. There were no ready meals. Housewives cooked from scratch most evenings, often using food that they had grown themselves. Now food frequently travels thousands of kilometres to reach your plate. Even food that could be grown locally is often imported.

THE GLOBAL FARM

One of the major causes of the food revolution has been changes in farming practices. Industrial-scale farming on a global scale has meant plentiful supplies to stock the supermarket shelves of the western world. Long-distance food shipments and more pre-prepared food have led to a greater use of packaging – UK households fill the equivalent of the Albert Hall in London with waste every hour. They have also introduced food additives – flavour enhancers and preservatives – to our diet.

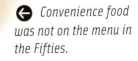 Convenience food was not on the menu in the Fifties.

WHAT'S THE DAMAGE?

Today, we have cheaper food and much more variety. What could be wrong with that? As food scares and crises constantly hit the headlines, more people are concerned that we are paying the price for food in different ways; that intensive farming and the chemicals we use to grow and make our food are damaging our health, wildlife and the environment. Are these people right? Does our food cost more than we think? Is it even safe to eat?

⬇ *What affects your choice of food at the supermarket?*

WHAT DO YOU THINK?

Before you consider some specific concerns about food safety and farming, ask yourself and your friends these questions.

- Would you describe your diet as healthy?
- Do you ever think about how much the food you eat costs?
- What problems do you think farmers face today?
- Do food scares in the news affect your eating habits?

MAXIMISING GROWTH

FOOD BECAME CHEAPER *when farms became more like factories. Bigger fields and bigger machines maximised efficiency. Artificial pesticides, fertilisers and new varieties of crops maximised yields.*

PESTICIDE FOR LUNCH?

Pesticides improve farmers' yields by killing off pests that damage their crops. Pesticides are, by definition, poisons and so can also kill harmless insects and other wildlife. This, in turn, affects the bigger birds and mammals further up the food chain that eat the smaller mammals. They have less food.

Traces of pesticide can also remain on the crop and are eaten by us. Some pesticides have been linked with serious diseases such as cancer.

GET THE FACTS STRAIGHT

Chemicals used in farming have different uses:
- **Fertilisers:** Provide nutrients which make plants grow better. Can be animal manure or factory-made.
- **Pesticides:** Poisons that kill plants and animals that might damage the crop.
- **Herbicides:** Pesticides that kill weeds.
- **Fungicides:** Pesticides that kill fungi that spoil crops.
- **Insecticides:** Pesticides that kill insects.

Industrial-scale farming has become standard practice. It has made food cheaper but has it made it safer?

PLANT FOOD

Fertilisers are not as dangerous. Farmers have used natural fertilisers – for example animal dung – for thousands of years. But today over 50 million tonnes of artificial fertiliser are used each year and it is this over-use that gives rise to concern.

Fertilisers can be washed off fields by the rain into lakes, rivers and reservoirs. This leaching causes aquatic plant life to grow excessively. Traces of the fertilisers can also end up in our drinking water. Some research has shown that, drunk in excess, the contaminated water can lead to a deadly illness in infancy called 'blue baby syndrome'.

Excessive plant growth such as this may be caused by fertilisers. When these plants die and rot, they will drain the oxygen from the river, killing animals that live in it.

Parents are often advised to peel fruit before giving it to children to avoid the pesticides in the skin.

WHO SAYS IT'S SAFE?

In most developed countries, governments decide how much fertiliser and pesticide can be used. In theory, they set the limits well below a level that might cause any harm.

Environmental groups such as Friends of the Earth say that these levels are just guesswork. They say we have no idea about the long-term effects of eating pesticides and are particularly worried about pesticides that belong to a group of chemicals called bio-accumulators. These are not destroyed when the food is eaten and build up in the body. Some of these chemicals have been linked to reproductive problems. Many environmentalists want all food to be pesticide-free.

ANIMAL PRODUCTION

People often become vegetarians rather than eating animals reared in conditions such as these.

IT IS NOT JUST plants that have become part of the industrial machine of farming today. Animals have too. And like plants, they have been dosed with chemicals to increase production. This has implications for food safety and, along with the conditions in which animals are raised, has highlighted issues of animal welfare.

HORMONE-HAPPY

Hormones are natural chemicals made by humans and other animals to control sexual development, reproduction and other functions. In the USA, Australia and other countries, cattle are given hormones to produce more milk or to make their meat less fatty.

But will the hormones act on the people who eat these products? The countries that use them say that the level of hormones is too low to make a difference. Others are less certain. The European Union (EU) has banned produce from hormone-enhanced animals. This followed public concern that the hormones might be causing cancer in sexual organs.

MEDICINE CHESTS

However, EU farmers are allowed to feed antibiotics – medicines used to kill germs – to their livestock on a regular basis. This is supposed to keep the animals free from disease. Antibiotics also help them to gain weight.

But regular doses of antibiotics can weaken the immune system – the mechanism the body uses to protect itself against germs. Some germs become resistant to antibiotics. There have been serious outbreaks of disease, for example among chickens, and there are fears about the impact of antibiotic use on human health. In 1983, 18 people in the USA suffered food poisoning caused by a drug-resistant bacteria. They had eaten beef from cows fed antibiotics. One person died.

CAGED IN

Animal welfare campaigners are concerned at the conditions in which many livestock are kept. For example, egg-laying hens are commonly kept five to a cage in a pen that measures just 50cm by 50cm. Compassion in World Farming (CiWF) says hens have been bred to grow twice as fast as they did 30 years ago and that this has led to leg problems and heart failure. Some places now sell food from animals reared in better conditions that have been independently checked by an animal-welfare expert.

FACING THE ISSUES

'It was the last straw for me,' said UK farmer Michael Bell. He was pumping his pigs with antibiotic to stop the brain disease, meningitis, from killing his herd, but he knew that the problem lay in the overcrowded conditions in which they were kept. The disease was being passed from pig to pig, just as a cold gets passed round a class at school. His farm was not an exception. This was standard practice for conventional farming – a system that he no longer wanted to be a part of. So Michael became an organic farmer.

← This sow and her piglets are 'free range'. Many people are prepared to pay extra for meat from animals raised in this way.

↘ In many countries, pigs are kept in stalls too small for them even to turn around. This practice is now banned in the UK.

BACK TO NATURE

MANY FARMERS HAVE *turned their backs on intensive, conventional farming and become organic farmers. Sales of their organic produce in the UK have grown by more than 25 per cent a year since 1995. There's a similar pattern worldwide. Organic farms are a friendlier place for wildlife – and its produce is healthier for us. At least, that's the claim...*

IT'S ONLY NATURAL

Birds, butterflies and meadow flowers are all victims of conventional farming's use of pesticides, the loss of hedges, and changes to the farming calendar. For example, farmland birds rely on stubble – left in the fields after the cereal crop has been harvested – as a source of winter food. But the drive for increased yields means that cereal crops are now planted in the winter rather than the spring and the stubble is ploughed up much earlier. This is thought to have caused big losses in bird numbers. The Soil Association, which promotes organic farming, found that organic farms had about 50 per cent more wild plants, insects and birds compared with conventional farms.

ORGANIC SHOPPING

Farmers who choose to go organic may do so from personal belief, but they are also responding to a rapidly growing market. Food scares about the use of pesticides, GM crops (see page 22), disease in meat (see page 16) and worries about animal welfare have caused more and more people to choose organic food. They may pay extra but feel it is worth it for peace of mind.

← *The 'gatekeeper' butterfly is one of many species whose numbers have dropped dramatically in the past 50 years. Organic farming may ensure its survival.*

Organic farmers avoid the use of pesticides. Campaigners say this makes their produce healthier.

SUPERMARKETS REACT

Supermarket shelves reflect this – in 2000, the Australian chain Coles increased its stock of organic food by 600 per cent. It is thought that by 2015, about 30 per cent of all food sold in the developed world will be organic.

ADDED VALUE?

Fans of organic food often claim it tastes different. To put this to the test, Consumer Report from the USA bought organic and conventional apples, carrots and tomatoes from farmers' markets and asked a panel if they could taste the difference. They couldn't. Similarly, tests carried out by the Consumers Institute of New Zealand failed to establish conclusively if organic food contained more nutrients. Other studies say organic food is more nutritious and does not contain pesticides. The arguments continue.

GET THE FACTS STRAIGHT

Organic farmers:

- don't routinely give animals antibiotics and other drugs
- ensure livestock has access to fresh air and sunlight
- avoid the use of artificial fertilisers and pesticides
- don't plant GM crops
- keep pests under control by encouraging their natural predators e.g. ladybirds and hoverflies which eat the pest insect, the aphid.

THE GLOBAL SUPERMARKET

NEXT TIME YOU are in a supermarket, check the labels to see where the food you choose comes from. A large part of it will probably come from abroad: in tins, dried, frozen or increasingly fresh, flown in from faraway places like Kenya, Chile or Thailand. This global supermarket has transformed farming and affected food safety.

STRAWBERRIES IN WINTER

The global trade in food gives customers the opportunity to eat food that would never grow in their country because of its climate, and also to eat food out of season – strawberries all year round! The EU now eats 95 times more imported food than it did 30 years ago and farmers now look to the export market for a large part of their profit. Australia relies on this trade. It produces far more food than it needs. Most of its rice, beef, sugar and wheat are exported.

⊗ *Assistants at an upmarket grocery proudly display their huge range of exotic fruit and produce.*

⊗ *In developed countries, strawberries, once summer treats, are now available all year round.*

→ *The transport of live animals raises concerns about animal welfare and the spread of diseases such as foot-and-mouth.*

QUALITY CONTROL

The worldwide exchange of food has also brought an exchange of diseases and constant battles to control this. Australia, for example, wants to ban imports of Canadian salmon because of the diseases they carry. In 2001, Britain faced an epidemic of foot-and-mouth disease, probably caused by the import of infected pig food.

SLAUGHTER POLICY

Foot-and-mouth is highly contagious and makes animals less productive, so, to stop the disease spreading, many countries banned British meat imports while the UK government slaughtered animals that might be infected. But, with animals being transported around so much, foot-and-mouth had already spread like wildfire. Millions of animals had to be killed. Now people are asking if international trade in meat and the movement of livestock should be limited to curb the spread of diseases in the future.

GET THE FACTS STRAIGHT

Preservatives stop food going bad. Food shipment makes their use essential. Here are some of the methods used:
- Salt, for example salt beef
- Vinegar, for example pickled onions
- Freezing, for example frozen peas
- Sugar, for example jams and fruit drinks
- Chemicals, known as E numbers. Their use is regulated but their safety is questioned.

FOLLOW THE HERD

Another focus of concern has been live animal transport. In 1998, almost 7 million pigs, nearly 3 million cattle and 2.5 million sheep were transported between EU countries. CiWF says it has examples of animals being kept in lorries in blistering heat without water. Even though welfare regulations exist, CiWF feels not enough is done to police them. It wants the live animal export trade stopped. Similar calls have been made in Australia where 5.8 million sheep and 800,000 cattle are transported live each year to Southeast Asia and the Middle East.

FOOD-BORNE DISEASES *are a major cause of illness. In the USA alone, it is estimated that they cause 76 million cases of sickness and 5,000 deaths a year. The US disease control service thinks they have a new and better way of protecting human health: food irradiation – zapping food with rays to kill germs – but not everyone agrees.*

GERM WARFARE

Most of us will suffer food poisoning in our lifetimes. The diarrhoea, vomiting and fever it causes can lead to death among vulnerable people such as the elderly and young children. In November 1996, 21 elderly people died in central Scotland from food poisoning caused by the bacterium E.coli O157, a type of germ. The bacterium is thought to have spread from a butcher's shop and to have made almost 500 people ill. Cases of E.coli poisoning have tripled in the last ten years.

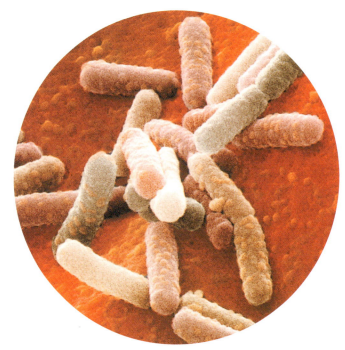

↑ *A close-up of the microscopic E.coli bacterium. E.coli outbreaks have been linked to contaminated beef, milk and vegetables.*

SALMONELLA POISONING

In 1994, a survey in the UK showed that four out of every ten frozen chickens carried another bacterium, salmonella. Measures were put in hand to reduce this. By 2001, just six out of every 100 chickens on sale in the UK were infected with salmonella. But a new problem had emerged, campylobacter, a bacterium that causes stomach pain and diarrhoea. One out of two chickens on sale was found to carry the bug.

← *Fruit and vegetables can also carry disease, particularly if they start to go mouldy. Claims that organic produce is more likely to be infected have not been proved.*

↗ *Food should be completely cooked before it is eaten. Supermarkets providing just-cooked meats have to be especially careful.*

WHAT CAN BE DONE?

Rules already exist on how to handle food hygienically, which has led some countries to consider using another weapon to tackle food poisoning: irradiation. Zapping food with gamma or X-rays kills bacteria – and so increases the shelf-life of fresh food. Some fruit is already irradiated in the USA; some spices are in the EU. But concerns about the safety of radiation have meant it has not been widely adopted. Now this is changing. The US government's disease control service thinks it is a way of protecting human health and the EU and Australia may expand the lists of food that can be irradiated. It will be a controversial decision as many worry about irradiation's long-term effects on human health.

WHAT DO YOU THINK?

Most experts agree that the best way to reduce food poisoning is to ensure people are taught how to handle food properly.

- Raw and cooked food should always be kept separate.
- Hands and cooking utensils should be washed when moving between the different types of food.
- Hands should be washed after going to the toilet.
- 'Use-by' dates should be respected. These are printed on the packaging of food that will go off. Once the 'use-by' date has passed, the foods should not be eaten.

Did you know these basic guidelines? Do you think you have enough hygiene education?

MAD COWS

FROM THE MID-1980s, *a crisis in UK farming and health has hit the headlines around the world: 'mad-cow' disease or BSE. It is now widely accepted that the use of intensive farming and meat production methods led to the spread of BSE and its human form, vCJD.*

MEAT FOR PLANT-EATERS

BSE disease was first identified in cattle in 1986. Most experts believe it was caused by farmers feeding cows, naturally plant-eaters, with pellets made from the meat and bone of animals infected with a prion disease (see panel). Farmers used these pellets because they were a cheap way of giving cattle protein to boost milk and meat yields. It takes four to six years for infected cattle to show the first signs of the BSE: clumsiness and disorientation.

Cows were fed pellets made from meat and bone to increase the milk and meat yields.

GET THE FACTS STRAIGHT

- Prion diseases: a group of diseases that attack the brain and nervous system of mammals.
- BSE (Bovine Spongiform Encephalopathy): a fatal prion disease of adult cattle. The brain tissue becomes spongy.
- CJD (Creutzfeldt-Jakob Disease): a rare prion disease that causes dementia in humans. It is fatal.
- vCJD (variant CJD): a new strain of CJD, which particularly affects young people. Its chemical profile suggest a strong link with BSE.

BSE TO vCJD

BSE is now thought to have caused vCJD in humans. Over 100 people have died of it in the UK and a few more in other EU countries. The disease probably passed to humans through MRM (mechanically-recovered meat), a method of meat production where the 'left-overs' of a carcass are squeezed to remove any edible material. It makes cheap meat for products such as burgers, sausages and pies.

No one knows for sure how many people may have contracted vCJD. Although some measures to stop BSE-infected beef being sold were already in place, it wasn't until 1996 that the Government admitted that there might be a serious risk to human health. It is now illegal in the UK to use or sell meat from a cow that has the slightest chance of being infected with BSE. Even certain parts of healthy cattle are banned from use.

Donna Marie McGivern died of vCJD in 1997. She was only seventeen years old.

The brain and spine of cattle – the parts most likely to harbour BSE – cannot be used in food. Butchers now have to be very careful.

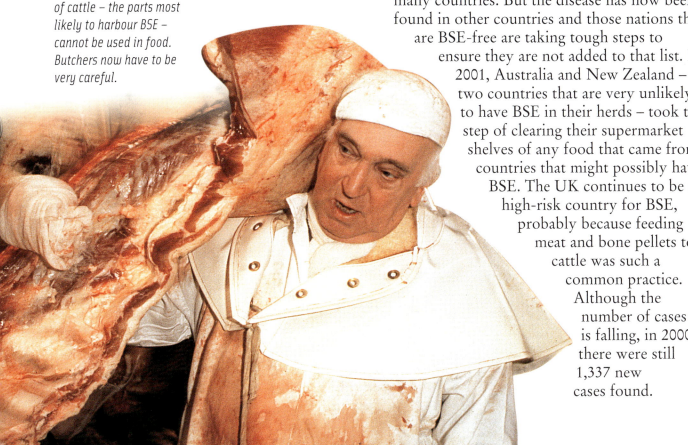

BANNED

The 1996 announcement caused a global reaction. UK beef exports were banned in many countries. But the disease has now been found in other countries and those nations that are BSE-free are taking tough steps to ensure they are not added to that list. In 2001, Australia and New Zealand – two countries that are very unlikely to have BSE in their herds – took the step of clearing their supermarket shelves of any food that came from countries that might possibly have BSE. The UK continues to be a high-risk country for BSE, probably because feeding meat and bone pellets to cattle was such a common practice. Although the number of cases is falling, in 2000 there were still 1,337 new cases found.

IN ANY SUPERMARKET *you can see shoppers filling their trolleys with packets of 16 toilet rolls and bags of 48 bread rolls. These people do not all come from large families, so why do they buy such big quantities? The answer is that it's cheaper to buy in bulk.*

THE BULK BUYERS

Supermarkets use the same principle. Over the years they have sought to buy larger quantities of food from fewer producers. The smaller, mixed farms of the Fifties could not provide the huge quantities that the supermarkets wanted – and they didn't have many alternative customers. By the mid-1990s just four supermarket chains sold more than half the food in the UK. Smaller farms began to go out of business, while the larger, specialist ones that emerged had to compete with farms all around the world. Intensive farming methods were adopted to keep the costs down.

↗ *Ever heard of a Blenheim Orange? Rare today, this variety of apple used to be widely available until the 1950s.*

NO VARIETY

One result of this is limited consumer choice. Name some apples. You may get stuck after Granny Smith's, Cox's, Golden Delicious and Braeburn, but there are hundreds of types of apple. We don't see them in the shops because supermarkets find it cheaper to sell just a handful of varieties.

'Farmers' markets' where only food from the local area is sold may help to save some of these varieties. These local markets also give shoppers the benefit of knowing exactly where their food is from and how it was produced.

← *Farmers today can expect to sell a calf for less than the price of a CD single.*

FAIR TRADE

Farmers in the developed world often complain that they sell their produce for less than it cost them to grow. This problem is even greater in developing countries, where middlemen control the paths to market and may work together to keep prices low.

Organisations, such as the Fairtrade Foundation, are working to ensure that poor farmers get a fair deal. You can see their logos in shops on goods from coffee and tea to bananas and chocolate. They usually cost a little more, but it is a way of shoppers helping farmers earn a decent living. Customer pressure has persuaded stores to stock these goods.

Tea was one of the first products to carry the Fairtrade mark, ensuring workers like these get a fairer share of the profits made from the sale of their crops.

GET THE FACTS STRAIGHT

Wal-Mart is the world's largest retailer.

- In 1998, it had global sales that were equal to one-tenth of the entire British economy.
- It has stores in Argentina, Brazil, Canada, Germany, Korea, Mexico, Puerto Rico and a special trading agreement in China. It bought ASDA stores, one of the UK's big four supermarkets, in 1998.
- It has 1.14 million employees worldwide.

FEED THE WORLD

BETWEEN THE 1960s and the 1990s, scientists and farmers tripled the amount of food grown. It was called the Green Revolution. As the world's population exploded, this food was badly needed. Are we producing enough food today? And who is controlling its production?

ENOUGH TO GO ROUND

In 1994, Norman E. Borlaug, often called the father of the Green Revolution, calculated that the planet was producing enough food for 6.4 billion people, 800 million more than the actual population, but millions were going hungry. And they still are today – even though some countries in the EU have so much food that their farmers are paid not to grow any more.

⬆ *Over 10 per cent of the Amazon rainforest has been cleared to make way for cattle ranches that supply meat to rich countries.*

WHY ARE PEOPLE STARVING?

People starve because food isn't always where it is needed. This may be due to war or natural disasters. However, people cannot always afford to buy the food that is available. In 1997, the World Bank reckoned that 1.3 billion people lived on a dollar (70p) or less a day. The problem is compounded when developing countries use their best agricultural land for 'cash' crops, such as tobacco or prime beef. They can export these for profits, most of which are either swallowed up by government debts or enrich a privileged few. If these crops are overproduced they can also exhaust the soil of nutrients, making the farmers dependent on chemical fertilisers and the land less productive in the future.

TRADE CONTROL

In 1995, the World Trade Organisation (WTO) was set up to promote international business, but many believe that it has too much power, not least over what we eat. The WTO believes people are better off because of its work to make trade between nations easier. It suggests, for example, that subsidies paid by governments to farmers should be reduced to make the trade fair to all farmers. But some people say the WTO is only concerned with profit and operates in the interests of big business – ignoring issues such as food safety and the problems facing individual farmers. Some governments argue that the subsidies are needed to control their food supply and protect their farmers and the environment.

FACING THE ISSUES

In 1999, a banana war broke out between the EU and the USA. The EU favoured bananas from its former colonies in the Caribbean and Africa over those from Central America. The EU believed that without their help the growers in the former colonies would go bankrupt, a disaster for such poor nations. The Americans claimed this argument was equally true of the Central American plantations (mostly US-controlled). The WTO said the ban was illegal, but the EU refused to back down. In retaliation, the US imposed £135m of trade sanctions on various EU exports. Eventually, after two and a half years, the EU gave in.

➡ *This boy and his family depend on the banana trade for their income. Like all of us, his life is affected by decisions made by the World Trade Organisation.*

FRANKENSTEIN FOODS

FRANKENSTEIN WAS A MAD *inventor who created a man-like monster who eventually killed him. Scientists have created GM foods, but many people are concerned that they will rebound on us – like Frankenstein.*

FAMILY TRAITS

GM foods come from plants and animals that have had their genes artificially altered. They are GMOs – genetically modified organisms. Genes tell the growing organism how to develop: what shape leaf to have or what colour fur to grow.

Scientists can identify the genes responsible for different characteristics. They can take them out of a living organism with that characteristic and put them into another organism at a very early stage in its life. It will then grow to have that characteristic: its genes will have been genetically engineered (GE) and we say the organism is transgenic. It could pass on those altered genes to the next generation.

KEEPING UP TRADITIONS?

Supporters of GM argue that this differs little from the practice of plant and animal breeders for the past thousand years: if a farmer wanted a litter of large piglets, he selected big pigs to mate with each other. Similarly, gardeners and agriculturalists had been creating hybrids of plants that would give more scented flowers or greater yields. But anti-GM campaigners say genetic engineering is different. It can pass genes between plant or animal species that would not normally breed together. They fear that we may be in for a nasty surprise.

⬇ *Friends of the Earth have made their point against GM with a Frankenstein monster called Genebeast.*

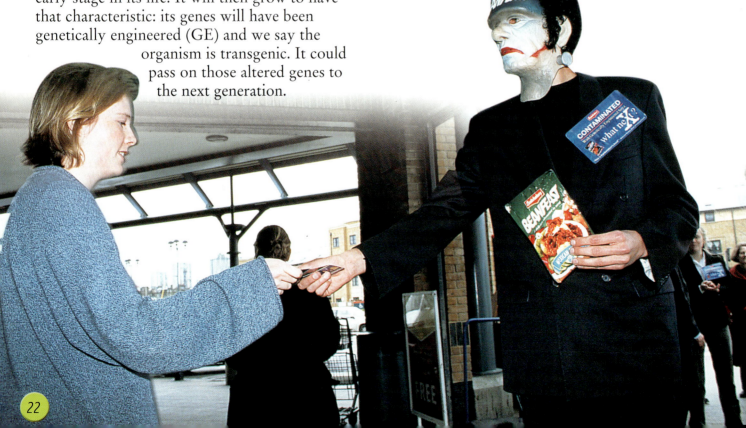

⤴ *All these different types of maize were created through hybrid techniques.*

➡ *Pollen blows from maize. Pollen from GM crops could spread in this way.*

A GROWING CONTROVERSY

Most of the world's GM crops are in the USA. In 1999, a third of the crops harvested in seven major farming states were transgenic. But this has hit US exports as consumer wariness of GM crops has grown. In the US, GM food does not generally have to be labelled as such, but this is not the case in many other nations and some of these have switched to other countries for their food imports. Farmers may want to swap back to conventional crops, but this may not be easy in areas where there are a lot of GM fields. GM plants could spread to non-GM fields through pollination, making a GM-free claim impossible. And consumers in the US could push for more comprehensive GM labelling too.

WHAT DO YOU THINK?

Many of the supporters of GM foods argue that it is a combination of media hype and ignorance that causes people to react so strongly against them.

- **Have you seen much about GM food in the news?**
- **What do you think of the media's coverage of the issue?**
- **What are your views on GM food now? Read on and see if they change...**

AN END TO STARVATION

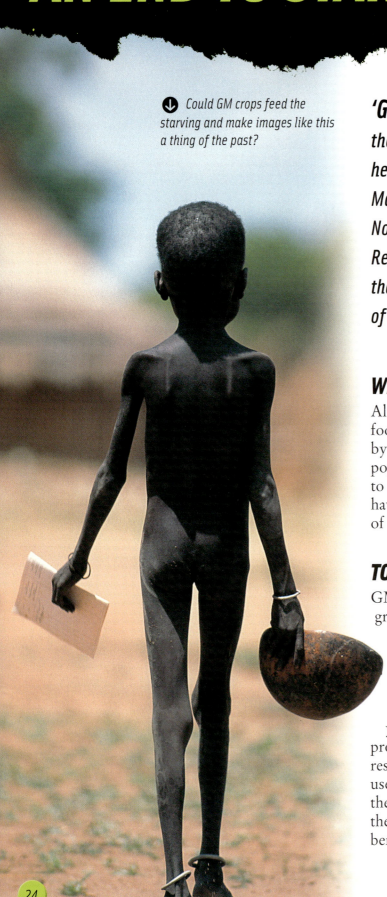

Could GM crops feed the starving and make images like this a thing of the past?

'GENE MANIPULATION *can help to feed the world. We must use this opportunity to help the starving.' So says Professor Malcolm Elliott, a genetic scientist from the Norman Borlaug Institute for Plant Science Research in the UK. If we don't, he believes that even rich countries will feel the effects of a world food shortage.*

WE NEED MORE

Although we are still increasing the amount of food that we produce, we are not increasing it by as much as we used to, and the global population continues to grow. If we are going to meet the demand for food in 2015, then we have to resort to GM – at least that is the view of Professor Elliott and other GM supporters.

TOUGH GUYS

GM techniques can alter plants so that they can grow in difficult conditions – such as drought areas or poor soils. Genes from a daffodil have enabled scientists to design a tomato that can survive in conditions as salty as the sea. Plants and animals can be made resistant to pests and diseases, improving yields. Some crops have even been altered to produce chemicals that kill pests. Others are resistant to herbicides, so herbicides can be used more effectively, killing the weeds and not the crop. All these genetic alterations reduce the need for fertiliser, herbicides and pesticides, benefiting the environment.

WHAT DO YOU THINK?

These are some of the main arguments for GM food. Do you think they are justified?

- It will help increase food production around the world, particularly in areas where the weather and soil conditions can badly affect the yields of traditional crops.

- It will reduce the need for pesticides and herbicides, and the chemicals that are needed will be more effective.

- GM foods are adequately tested to ensure their safety.

- There is no existing evidence that GM crops have harmed humans or wildlife.

- Interbreeding in traditional farming methods is also a form of GE.

The Flavr Savr tomato was one of the first GM foods in the supermarkets, but shoppers did not go out of their way to buy it.

NUTRITIOUS NOSH

With GM, crops can be made more nutritious. A type of rice has been made that contains vitamin A, one of the essential ingredients of a healthy diet. A lack of vitamin A is thought to have caused 500,000 children to go blind in the mid-90s.

Waste can be cut down as well. For example, the GM Flavr Savr tomato stays firmer longer – so fewer are damaged in transit. Finally, along with all the benefits, says the GM lobby, testing of new GM crops is thorough and there is no evidence that they have harmed humans or wildlife.

BUSINESS, NOT THE STARVING, *will benefit from GM food, say its opponents. They claim a few big companies will control the world's agriculture and will be able to dictate prices for seed and pesticides. They also say that too little is known about the long-term effect of GM food on the environment and our health. It's a 'great food gamble' says Friends of the Earth.*

BURNING ISSUE

GM supporters often claim that their opponents are people from rich countries who are spoilt for choice when it comes to food. But GM protests have not been confined to industrialised countries. In 1998, Indian farmers set fire to a trial field of cotton when they found out that it was GM. They fear that they will have to pay more to use GM crops because of GURTs (Genetic Use Restriction Technology).

⬇ *These farmers in Bangladesh don't believe GM crops will help them.*

HELD TO RANSOM

GURTs can stop farmers saving seed from their crop to plant the following year, a common method in poor areas. GM companies say this practice weakens the crop. One of them, Monsanto, wanted to insert a 'terminator gene' into one of its GM crops to make it infertile. This would have stopped farmers putting aside seed, but it caused such an outcry that the company backed down.

Some GM companies have tried to take out patents (legal ownership) on useful naturally-occurring gene sequences. Will they then be able to charge farmers to plant crops that they have grown for generations? And there are concerns about food allergies. Procedures exist to stop genes that cause an allergy from being used to modify another crop, but are they good enough?

⬇ *Protestors destroy a field of GM crops – but are they acting out of selfishness and ignorance?*

WHAT DO YOU THINK?

The GM debate raises a huge number of complicated questions. For example:

- Who will really profit: the starving or the biotech companies?
- What will happen if a gene that has made a crop poisonous to a pest is transferred to wild plants? Will the animals that eat the wild plants be poisoned?
- What if the gene for herbicide tolerance is passed to weeds? Could 'superweeds' be created?
- What will be the effect on humans of eating GM food over many years?
- Given all the unknowns, is it worth the risk?

ANTI-SCIENCE VANDALS

Anti-GM protestors fear that modified genes will spread from GM crops to wild plants through wind and insect pollination – with unknown effects on wild plants and the animals that live on them. They have destroyed several trial sites of GM crops, set up so that scientists can learn more about GM. As a result, they have been accused of being anti-science vandals who have ended the very experiments that could answer their questions.

WHAT DOES THE rest of this century hold for farming? It would astound those Fifties housewives to learn that the next big change may have nothing to do with food.

⬆ *These baby mice are transgenic. They have been given a gene from a jellyfish that makes them fluorescent!*

⬆ *What we choose to eat affects our health and the future of farming.*

THE FUTURE OF PHARMING

'Pharming' – pharmaceutical farming – looks set to be the next agricultural revolution. Animals with human genes could be used as factories for making medicines and organs that can be transplanted into human patients. Three US companies are racing to be the first to add human genes to chickens so that they produce human chemicals, such as insulin (used to treat diabetes), in their eggs. Tobacco plants have been altered to produce vaccines and antibodies that protect the body from germs. These vegetable versions have been nicknamed 'plantibodies' and can be produced much more cheaply than in the laboratory.

PROBLEMS TO COME

The other big issue of the coming decades is water. You can't grow anything without it. Underground water reservoirs – aquifers – are depleted in many areas because they have been used too much; and in some cases they are contaminated by pesticides and fertilisers. With the world's population growing and the global climate changing, the situation looks even more worrying. Water shortages already underlie some of the worst conflicts in the world today: in the Middle East and Rwanda, for example.

WHAT DO YOU THINK?

So the future of food seems to revolve around these questions:

- What can we do to end hunger?
- Can technology help?
- Is more global trade the answer or would it be better if each country grew as much of its own food as possible?
- And who can we trust to tell us if our food is safe?

The answers will be served to you on a plate in the coming decades.

⬇ *Riots occurred in Genoa in 2001 when people protested against the globalisation of business, including farming.*

LIFESTYLES

What we will eat in the future does not just depend on governments and business. Fast food has become a way of life because people want tasty food in a hurry. Organic food has boomed because people are worried by repeated food scares. People change the food industry through their choices about what to eat and with that power comes responsibility.

At the same time, campaigners for food safety and good farming practice recognise that many issues are linked with other concerns – the preservation of the environment, the morality of manipulating nature, the domination of international business in our everyday lives. These too affect our decisions about what we eat and how we farm.

GLOSSARY

additives: Chemicals added to food to stop it going off or to improve its colour or flavour. Salt, sugar, and corn syrup are among the most common.

biotech: Short for biotechnology, which is the science of using our knowledge of living organisms to meet practical needs.

BSE: Stands for Bovine Spongiform Encephalopathy, a disease that affects adult cattle. BSE attacks the brain and nervous system of the animal and leads to death.

European Union (EU): A group of European countries that have come together to encourage trade and to develop closer political ties. They have many laws in common.

fertiliser: a substance that contains plant nutrients and is used to encourage plant growth. It can be natural (e.g. manure) or artificial.

foot-and-mouth: A highly contagious disease of various animals characterised by blisters in the mouth and on the feet.

gene: A set of instructions held within the cells of an organism that enables it to reproduce itself in the next generation.

genetically engineered (GE): See genetically modified.

genetically modified (GM): Describes a plant or animal that has had its genes altered. A GMO is a genetically modified organism. The term genetically engineered (GE) is also used.

herbicide: A chemical designed to kill weeds.

hormone: A chemical produced naturally by an animal. It triggers changes in the body.

hybrid: Describes plants and animals which have been created by crossing two different species.

infertile: Unable to reproduce.

insecticide: A chemical designed to kill insects.

livestock: Farm animals.

nutrients: The different food materials that organisms need to grow and stay healthy.

organic farming: A way of farming that uses natural processes to boost yields.

organism: A living thing.

pesticide: A chemical designed to kill pests e.g. certain insects and plants, rats or mice.

pollination: The process by which many plants reproduce. The pollen from a male flower must pass to the female flower for seeds to form. Pollen is usually carried between flowers by insects or the wind.

population: The number of a particular type of plant or animal, including humans.

protein: A nutrient found in meat, milk, eggs, nuts and seeds. Essential for muscle growth.

shelf-life: The length of time a food item can be sold (or displayed on a shop's shelf).

species: A type of plant or animal.

transgenic: Describes an organism whose genes have been altered by introducing genes from another species using genetic engineering.

vaccine: A drug that produces resistance to disease.

vCJD: Stands for variant Creutzfeldt-Jakob Disease, a new type of CJD that is thought to be caused by people eating beef infected with BSE. CJD is a form of dementia where people lose their ability to concentrate and to control their bodies. It is fatal.

FURTHER INFORMATION

INTERNATIONAL ORGANISATIONS

Food and Agriculture Organisation of the United Nations
Regional Office for Europe
Viale delle Terme di Caracalla
00100 Rome
Italy

Regional Office for North America
2175 K Street NW, Suite 300
Washington, DC 20437
USA

Regional Office for Asia and the Pacific
Maliwan Masion
39 Phra Atit Rd
Bangkok, 10200
Thailand
www.fao.org

World Trade Organisation
Centre William Rappard
Rue de Lausanne 154
CH-1211 Geneva 21
Switzerland
www.wto.org

INDEPENDENT ORGANISATIONS AND PRESSURE GROUPS

Compassion in World Farming
Charles House
5A Charles Street
Petersfield
Hants, GU32 3EH
UK
www.ciwf.co.uk

Consumers' Institute of New Zealand Inc (CINZ)
Private Bag 6996
Wellington 6030
New Zealand
www.consumer.org.nz

The Fairtrade Foundation
Suite 204
16 Baldwin's Gardens
London
EC1N 7RJ
UK
www.fairtrade.org.uk

Monsanto Company
800 North Lindbergh Blvd
St. Louis, MO 63167
USA
www.monsanto.com

Friends of the Earth
International Secretariat
P.O. Box 19199
1000 GD Amsterdam
The Netherlands
www.foei.org

The Royal Society
6 Carlton House Terrace
London SW1Y 5AG
UK
www.royalsociety.org

Soil Association
Bristol House
Victoria Street
Bristol
BS1 6BY
UK
www.soilassociation.org

GOVERNMENT AGENCIES

European Commission
200 rue de la Loi/Wetstraat 200
B-1049 Brussels
Belgium
www.europa.eu.int/comm/food

Food Standards Agency
Room 245
Aviation House
125 Kingsway
London
WC2B 6NH
UK
www.foodstandards.gov.uk

Australia New Zealand Food Authority
PO Box 7186
Canberra Mail Centre
ACT 2610
Australia

PO Box 10559
The Terrace
Wellington 6036
New Zealand
www.anzfa.gov.au

United States Department of Agriculture
14th & Independence Ave SW
Washington
DC 20250
USA
www.usda.gov/vistor/vistor.htm

INDEX